Mapping Britain's Landscapes

Coasts

Barbara Taylor

FRANKLIN WATTS
LONDON•SYDNEY

COASTAL SAFETY

Coasts can be dangerous places. Always follow the safety advice of a teacher or other adult, take care on slippery rocks, stay away from the edge of cliffs and make sure you are not cut off by the tide.

First published in 2007 by Franklin Watts

Copyright © Franklin Watts 2007

Franklin Watts
338 Euston Road
London NW1 3BH

Franklin Watts Australia
Level 17/207 Kent Street
Sydney, NSW 2000

Series editor: Sarah Peutrill
Art director: Jonathan Hair
Design: Jason Billin
Series design: White Design
Consultant: Steve Watts
Picture research: Diana Morris
Additional map illustrations: John Alston

A CIP catalogue record for this book is available from the British Library.

Dewey number: 526.09141
ISBN: 978 0 7496 7113 6

Printed in China

Franklin Watts is a division of Hachette Children's Books, an Hachette Livre UK company.

Picture credits: Stephen Almond/Geoffrey Pass Photography/PD: 12. Neil Beer/Corbis: 1, 11. Comisiwn Brenhinol Henebion Cymu/Royal Commission on the Ancient & Historical Monuments of Wales: 24. Geogphoto/Alamy: 25. Joe Gough/Shutterstock: 7. Chinch Gryniewicz/Corbis: 16. Jason Hawkes/Corbis: front cover r, 5, 23. Andrew Holt/Alamy: 15. Roger Howard/PD: 19. © Maps.com/Corbis: 20. Ordnance Survey © Crown copyright 2007: front cover l. Ordnance Survey © Crown copyright 2007 supplied by mapsinternational.co.uk: 4, 9, 10,13, 14, 17, 18, 21, 22, 29. Nick Wheeler/Corbis: 8.
Every attempt has been made to clear copyright. Should there be any inadvertent omission please apply to the publisher for rectification.

Contents

Mapping coasts

The coastline around Britain stretches for some 19,300 kilometres and no place in Britain is more than 121 kilometres from the coast.

HUGE VARIETY

This meeting place between the land and the sea includes a huge variety of scenery, from tall, rugged cliffs and rocky islands to muddy salt marshes and beaches of golden sand. Coasts are always changing shape as the sea wears away the land in some places, carrying the material away to build up new land in other places.

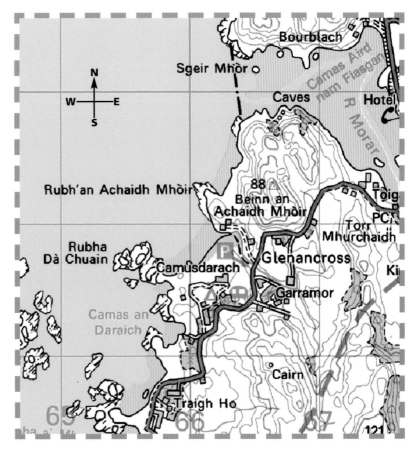

↓ What are maps?

Maps are usually flat drawings of places seen from above, as if you were a bird looking down from the sky. This aerial view means that all the features can be seen clearly at the same time. Maps are also simplified versions of the real world, which mark important pieces of information chosen by the map-maker. These are marked by symbols on the map (see page 10). Maps give much more information than photographs and can be used in a variety of ways, such as to help tourists plan a holiday, to plan coastal defences or to develop seaside towns.

Map Symbols (Key)

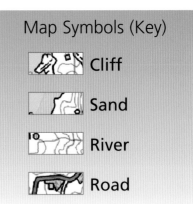

Cliff

Sand

River

Road

↑ **This photo shows part of the beautiful coastline of north-west Scotland, near Morar, Mallaig and the Isle of Skye. Cliffs and caves show where the sea is wearing away the land and beaches show where material is being added to the land.**

Look at the photo and the map

→ **Can you match up the photo with the map? (You may need to turn the book upside down so the sea is on the right of the map.)**

→ **Find the hilly area Beinn an Achaidh Mhóir and the trees that grow right down to the beach near the caves. How many sandy beaches are marked on the map? How are the flat rocks on the coastal edge of the hill marked on the map?**

TAKING IT FURTHER

Using an atlas, compare the shape of the coastline in the west of Britain with that in the east. How are the coastlines different? Look at the height of the cliffs and see where you can find areas of salt marshes and mudflats. The older, harder rocks on the west coast are exposed to the westerly winds and form a jagged shape. The softer rocks on the sheltered east coast form a smoother, more rounded coastline of low, crumbling cliffs with large areas of mud or sand dunes.

Wearing away coasts

The coast is shaped by the force of the wind, rain and the waves. They constantly attack the shore, breaking up the rocks and eating into the land. This process of wearing away the rocks is called erosion. The amount of erosion depends partly on the type of rocks along the coast.

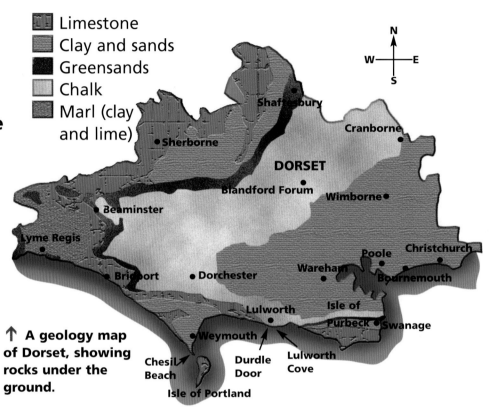

Limestone
Clay and sands
Greensands
Chalk
Marl (clay and lime)

Shaftesbury
Cranborne
Sherborne
DORSET
Blandford Forum
Wimborne
Beaminster
Lyme Regis
Poole
Christchurch
Wareham
Bridport
Dorchester
Bournemouth
Isle of
Lulworth
Purbeck
Swanage
Weymouth
Chesil
Beach
Durdle
Door
Lulworth
Cove
Isle of Portland

↑ A geology map of Dorset, showing rocks under the ground.

COASTAL EROSION

Waves erode the coast in five main ways.
- The waves pound against the coast and tear it apart.
- Waves hurl sand and pebbles against the shore, cutting into the rocks and making pieces break off.
- Pieces of rock grind against each other, becoming smaller and smoother.
- Seawater forces its way into cracks in the rocks, squashing pockets of air into small spaces. When the wave pulls back, the air expands and explodes, bursting the rocks apart.
- The chemicals in seawater dissolve certain rocks, particularly chalk and limestone.

SHAPING THE COASTLINE

Soft rocks along the coast are worn away faster than hard rocks to form circular bays. Harder rocks stick out into the sea to form headlands. Sometimes the waves slowly eat away at the base of a cliff, forming a cave. If caves form on opposite sides of a headland, they may eventually meet in the middle to form a natural stone arch. If the top of the arch collapses, it leaves a pillar of rock called a stack. In time, the stack will eventually be eroded away.

↓ **The photo shows a natural rock arch called Durdle Door, which is on the Dorset coast just west of Lulworth Cove.**

Look at the photo and the map

→ This Dorset coastline is an important World Heritage Site because it has a variety of coastal features close together in a small area.

→ If you look carefully at the geology map, you will see the reason for this is that bands of several different kinds of rock end at the coastline. (Each type of rock is a different colour.)

→ At Durdle Bay, most of the hard limestone rock has been eroded away, leaving just the small headland with its famous arch. Soft rocks behind the limestone are now exposed to the full force of the waves and have been worn away to form a bay.

TAKING IT FURTHER

• Find an Ordnance Survey Map of the Dorset coast and look for Durdle Door and Lulworth Cove.
• What are the names of some of the other bays along this coastline? What are the caves on Durlston Head called?
• Find Old Harry Rocks on the coast of the Isle of Purbeck. These chalk arches and stacks were once joined to the chalk stacks called The Needles on the Isle of Wight.

Cliffs

At the coast, the land may end in a gentle slope or a towering wall of rock and soil called a cliff. The highest sea cliffs on mainland Britain are on the northern tip of Scotland at Clo Mor. They are 281 metres high.

 These are the tall chalk cliffs of Beachy Head, which is on the south coast of England, near Eastbourne. The people on the top of the cliff give you some idea of its height, which is 162 metres, making it the highest chalk sea cliff in Britain. From the top of the cliff it is possible to see towns such as Eastbourne and Brighton and even, on a very clear day, the Isle of Wight.

COLLAPSING CLIFFS

The size and angle of the cliff depends on the type of rock and how easily it can be worn away by the pounding of the waves. If the bottom of a cliff is eroded by the waves, it may become unstable and collapse. Over many years, the whole coastline may retreat inland as the cliffs collapse over and over again.

↓ Using the map

Cliffs on maps

On a map, cliffs are usually marked by a thin strip of jagged black lines. You may also see thick black lines called hachures, which show steep slopes.

The other way of finding out about the steepness of the land near the coast is to look at the brown lines called contours. These lines join up points on the map that are the same height above sea level. They are spaced at regular intervals, such as 10 metres. When the contour lines are close together, it shows that the land is very steep. The land increases in height very quickly over a small area. When the contour lines are further apart, it shows that the land slopes more gently.

- On the map below, where are the contours close together? Where are the contours further apart?
- Find the blue line at the bottom of the cliff. This shows the highest point reached by the seawater (high water mark).
- The circle of blue lines marks the viewpoint where people go to see the best views.

TAKING IT FURTHER

- Compare the cliffs at Beachy Head with the famous 'White Cliffs' of Dover. See if you can find out what chalk is made from.
- How high are the Dover cliffs?
- How far away is the coast of France?
- How long does it take to travel from Dover to France on a ferry?

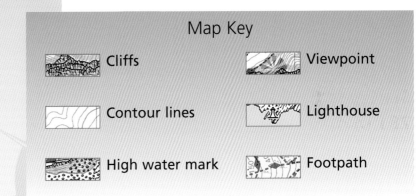

Map Key

	Cliffs		Viewpoint
	Contour lines		Lighthouse
	High water mark		Footpath

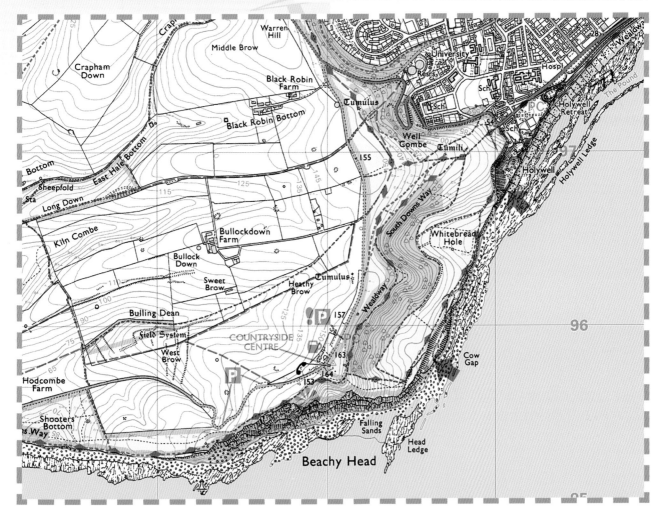

Beaches and dunes

As waves erode the coast, the rocks are eventually broken up into pebbles, shingle and sand. Some of this material is swept out to sea, but some is washed up, or deposited, in sheltered bays or along strips of land on the edge of the sea. Over time, this material builds up to form beaches and may pile up into low hills of sand called dunes.

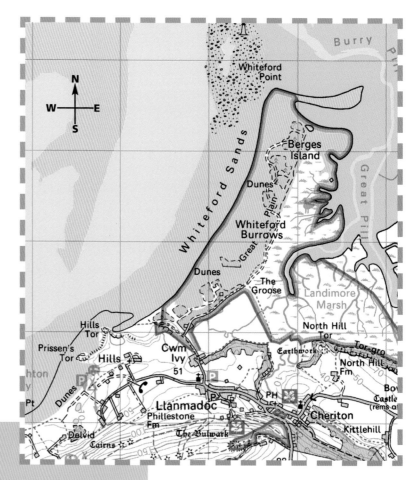

↓ Using the map

Symbols

There is not room to draw detailed pictures of everything on a map. Instead, simple signs, called symbols, show where things are. Bold shapes, letters, lines or coloured areas stand for natural features, such as sand dunes and man-made features, such as lighthouses. Rocky beaches are marked with pictures of little rocks. A list called a key on the edge of a map explains what the symbols mean.

Look at the key to the map of Whiteford Burrows and find the things listed in the key.

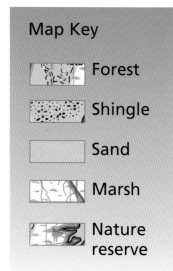

Map Key

Forest

Shingle

Sand

Marsh

Nature reserve

↑ **The sandy beach of Whiteford Burrows, in South Wales.**

TYPES OF BEACHES

The size of beach material depends on things such as the type of rock and how powerful the waves are.

- Pebbles are formed when the sea rolls pieces of rock around until the corners are smooth and rounded. Large, heavy pebbles are often dropped at lower levels on the beach, while small, light pebbles are carried further by the waves.
- Over millions of years, stony beaches may turn into sandy ones as pebbles or shingle are ground up into tiny grains of sand. (Sand itself is sharp and rubs away at pebbles, helping to wear them away.)
- Some beaches, such as Mochras in Wales, are made of tiny pieces of crushed shells, which once covered the bodies of shellfish such as cockles. Shell beaches often have very white sand.
- Storm beaches are ridges of boulders, which stormy seas pile up near the top of the beach.

Look at the photo

→ **This spectacular sandy beach is three kilometres long. Behind the beach, the winds have blown some of the sand into high sand dunes, with ridges at right angles to the direction of the wind. Dunes can only form on coasts with low slopes next to the shore.**

TAKING IT FURTHER

- Compare the dunes on the west coast of Britain with those on the east coast. Which coast has narrow dunes and which coast has wider, more spread out dunes?
- Find maps of large dune systems, such as Braunton Burrows in North Devon or Newborough Warren on the island of Anglesey, North Wales. The biggest sand dune system in Britain is Culbin Sands, in Scotland, which covers 3,100 hectares. Can you find Culbin Sands on a map? How high are the tallest dunes at Culbin Sands?

11

Changing shape

Sand, mud, pebbles and other loose material deposited on the coast is sometimes pulled along sideways by the waves. This is called longshore drift. If there is a break in a coastline, longshore drift may push the loose material out into the sea. The flow of water slows down and material is deposited to form long, thin ridges called bars, spits or tombolos, which change the shape of the coastline.

SPITS, BARS AND TOMBOLOS

- A spit is a curved beach of sand and pebbles that is joined to the land at one end but sticks out into the sea. A spit with a curved end is called a recurved spit.
- If a spit grows right across a bay, or the mouth of a river, it is called a bar. A shallow area of freshwater called a lagoon may be trapped behind a bar, as at Slapton Sands in Devon.
- A tombolo is a ridge of material linking an island to the mainland. One end of Chesil Beach is a tombolo joining the Isle of Portland to the mainland of Dorset (see page 6).

↓ Spurn Head is a spit at the mouth of the Humber Estuary, in Yorkshire. It is about 5.5 kilometres long. Compare the photo with the map on the right hand side of page 13. Can you see that the spit is above the thick blue line marking the highest point reached by the sea?

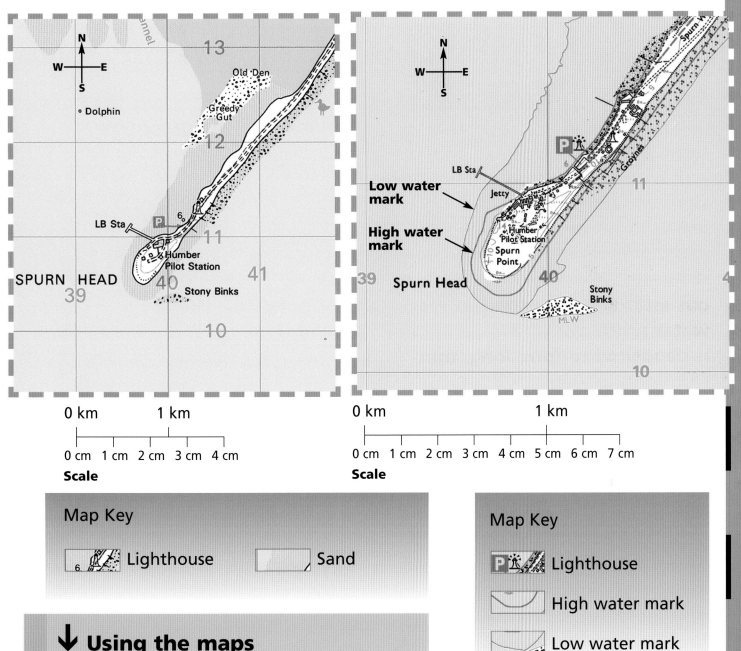

0 km   1 km

0 cm   1 cm   2 cm   3 cm   4 cm

Scale

0 km   1 km

0 cm   1 cm   2 cm   3 cm   4 cm   5 cm   6 cm   7 cm

Scale

Map Key

Lighthouse	Sand

Map Key

Lighthouse	
High water mark	
Low water mark	

⬇ Using the maps

Scale

The two maps of Spurn Head are drawn at different scales. The smaller scale map (left) shows a larger area of the spit with less detail. The larger scale map (right) shows a small area of the spit in more detail. The scale on each map shows how many kilometres on the real spit are represented by a certain number of centimetres on the map. Use the scale to work out the distance from the lighthouse to the south end of the spit on both maps.

TAKING IT FURTHER

Look for maps of some other spits, such as Hurst Castle spit on the Hampshire coast or Orford Ness on the Suffolk coast. Use the scale on these maps to work out the size of each spit. Compare the size with that of Spurn Head. Which is the biggest spit you can find?

Where rivers meet coasts

Coasts are frontiers between the freshwater in rivers and the salty water in the sea. The water mixes together in estuaries, where rivers flow into the sea and seawater moves up and down the estuaries with the tides. Estuaries are full of the mud and sand deposited by rivers. This mud may build up into a salt marsh if plants grow on the mud and stop it from being washed away.

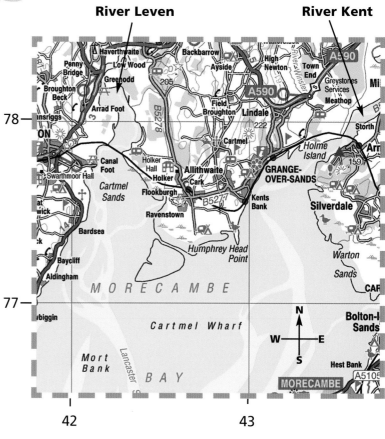

River Leven   River Kent

WHY ESTUARIES ARE IMPORTANT

There are more than 150 large estuaries around the coasts of Britain. They are important for a number of reasons:

- They are home to a rich variety of wildlife.
- They are good sites for ports and marinas because they are sheltered from the full force of the sea.
- Power stations are often built on estuaries since they need a good supply of water.
- Flood barriers may be built across estuaries to control flooding further up the river.

↓ Using the map

Grid references

A map of Morecambe Bay may seem rather confusing. A series of squares drawn on top of a map divides it into sections, making it easier to find things. These squares are called grid squares and the lines are called grid lines. At the end of each grid line is a number. The grid reference for the bottom left-hand corner of a particular square is the number of

River
Leven

River
Kent

River
Lune

River
Wyre

↑ **This aerial photograph shows the rivers that feed into Morecambe Bay.**

Look at the photo and the map

→ **Morecambe Bay in north-west England is the meeting place of four river estuaries – the Leven, the Kent, the Lune and the Wyre. The wide, shallow bay covers an area of 310 square kilometres and is the largest area of sandflats and mudflats in Britain. The bay is a dangerous area because the tides cover the sand and mud very quickly and there are large areas of quicksands. Guided walks of the bay show people the safe paths across the bay.**

the line at the top or bottom of the map, followed by the number of the line at the sides. Remember the phrase, "along the corridor and up the stairs". For instance Ravenstown is in 4277. In which grid square are Holme Island and Warton Sands?

TAKING IT FURTHER

Up to 200,000 people live and work around Morecambe Bay. Find out more about it. For example:
- What natural resources provide jobs in the area?
- Find out about the natural gas reserves under the sea just beyond the entrance to the bay.
- Which chemical companies have factories in the area?
- How important is tourism to the local economy?

Coastal settlements

From sheltered harbours and cliff-top forts to trade routes and tourist locations, the coast has always been a good place for people to settle. Small fishing villages have sometimes grown into large coastal cities, especially where natural resources such as coal, stone or metals are found near the coast.

↓ Swansea in South Wales is a coastal city with a population of around 220,000.

WHY LIVE NEAR COASTS?
- Food can be taken from the sea and along the shore.
- Rich lowland farmland often occurs near the coast.
- Cliffs and estuaries can be defended from attack.
- Transport is available by sea along the coast and inland along rivers that flow into the sea.
- Power stations need lots of cooling water, which the sea can provide. Wind and wave power can also be generated on the coast.
- Coasts have beautiful beaches and other spectacular scenery so people often choose to live there, or retire there, or just stay for their holidays.

Look at the photo and the map

→ This photograph of Swansea in South Wales on the opposite page was taken from the Mayhill area. Find this on the map. The settlement grew up at the mouth of the River Tawe and its Welsh name is *Aber-tawe*, meaning 'at the mouth of the Tawe'. The town first developed as a market town and port but expanded greatly in the 17th and 18th centuries due to the export of coal by sea. Metal smelting works, especially for copper, led to the growth of population and housing in the 19th century. Traditional industries declined in the 20th century and today, light industries and a waterfront and leisure park have taken the place of heavy industry. What evidence can you see for this on the map?

↓ Using the map

Leisure symbols
See what you can discover about Swansea today by looking at the symbols on the map. Why do you think the windmill was built where it is?

TAKING IT FURTHER
Find some maps of other coastal towns and cities in South Wales, such as Newport, Cardiff, Port Talbot, Llanelli, Tenby and Pembroke. How are they similar and different? Which is the largest town or city? How did each town or city grow up? What are the main industries today?

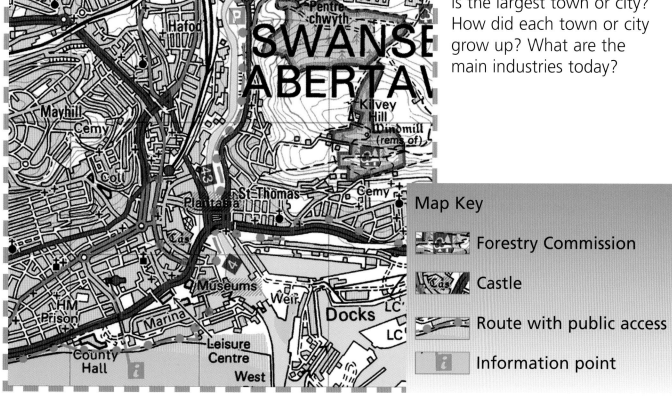

Map Key

Forestry Commission

Castle

Route with public access

Information point

Ports and harbours

Many harbours are naturally sheltered areas on the coast that can be used for loading and unloading cargo and passengers from boats. A harbour does not always have the means to transfer cargo but a port always has these facilities.

NATURAL OR BUILT

Some harbours, such as Dover, are built by people, with breakwaters providing shelter from the wind and waves. Even natural harbours often need to be made larger and deeper to make room for huge cargo ships. The ports at London, Bristol and Glasgow all developed because they could be reached by large cargo ships.

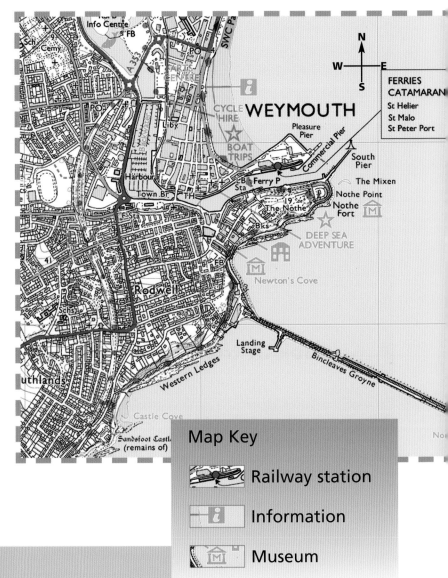

FERRIES
CATAMARAN
St Helier
St Malo
St Peter Port

Map Key

Railway station

Information

Museum

⬇ Look at the map

Compass points

On a map, an arrow usually points to the direction of north. This is usually at the top of the map, while south is at the bottom, west is on the left and east is on the right. (West and east always spell the word 'we'.)

Is Nothe Fort on the east or the west of the map? Is the Pleasure Pier to the north or the south of the Commercial Pier? What is the name of the district to the south of the Town Bridge? Is the railway station on the north side or the south side of the harbour entrance?

Look at the photo

→ Weymouth, at the mouth of the River Wey, has been a port for many centuries. In Roman times, ships sailed up the River Wey as far as Radipole to unload cargo bound for the town of Dorchester. During the Second World War (1939–45), the whole population of Alderney was evacuated through Weymouth harbour because of the German invasion of the Channel Islands.

→ Even though the port is small, it still has a fishing fleet and takes passenger ferries to the Channel Islands. In Weymouth's inner harbour are modern marina facilities for leisure boats.

↑ This view of Weymouth, on the Dorset coast, was taken from the harbour bridge.

TAKING IT FURTHER

Compare a map of Dover with a map of Weymouth. Dover is the world's busiest passenger port and the main port for people crossing the English Channel to France. The harbour is divided into three main areas: the outer harbour, the west docks and the east docks. How is this different from Weymouth? Is there a river flowing into the sea at Dover as there is at Weymouth?

Tourism and leisure

Coastal tourism and the leisure industry have transformed Britain's coastal towns, allowing them to rely less on the traditional industries such as fishing. Unfortunately, large numbers of seaside visitors tend to cause pollution problems and damage coastal wildlife.

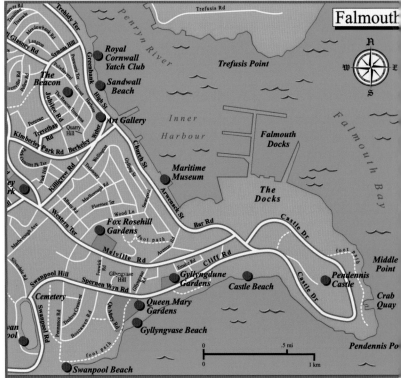

MANY FACILITIES

Apart from all the hotels, marinas, campsites and the services that go with them, there are theme parks, funfairs, theatres, cinemas and nightclubs to provide entertainment for visitors on holiday. Some larger resorts have conference centres to attract visitors throughout the year.

PEOPLE PROBLEMS

Tourists cause all sorts of problems for coastal environments.

- Small coastal towns with narrow streets are often choked with cars and people in the summer. Park-and-ride schemes help to ease this congestion.
- Caravan sites on cliff-tops and large numbers of people on beaches disturb nesting seabirds.
- People leave litter on beaches and the sewage from coastal towns or oil spills from ships may pollute the seawater. Look out for resorts that have won blue flag awards for having clean beaches and providing facilities and safety measures.
- People walking along the coast erode fragile sand dunes and the thin soils on cliff-tops.

↓ Look at the two maps

Look carefully at the two maps of Falmouth, Cornwall. Falmouth has four lovely beaches, cliff-top walks and many places of interest, such as Pendennis Castle (built by Henry VIII) and the Cornwall Maritime Museum. It also has the third largest natural harbour in the world.

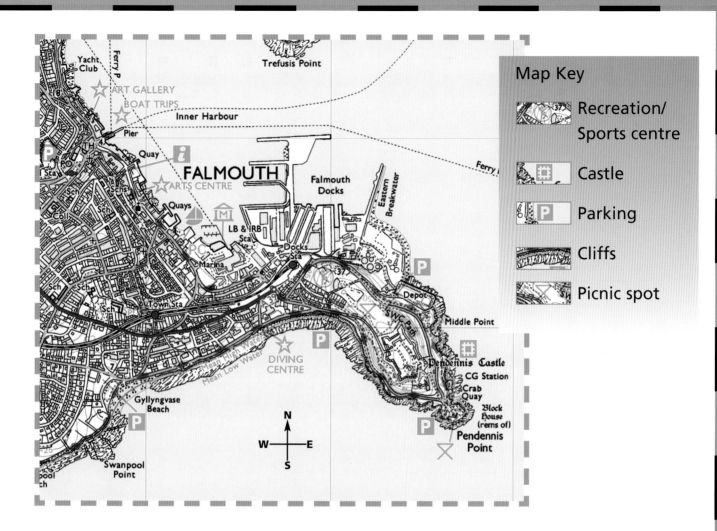

Tourist maps, like the map on the left, are different from landscape maps, such as Ordnance Survey maps. They focus on the locations of tourist sites, such as museums, castles, gardens and beaches.

Tourist maps usually include the road names but do not include landscape details, such as contours, the shape of cliffs or high and low water lines. On the whole, tourist maps are simpler and less cluttered than landscape maps, making it easier for tourists to find places they are looking for.

Can you find three things on the Ordnance Survey map that are not on the tourist map? Compare the symbols on the two maps. How are they different?

TAKING IT FURTHER

Draw a map showing how to get from the Art Gallery in Falmouth to Swanpool Beach and Pendennis Castle. Use both maps to help you. Colour in the roads you would need to take and use the scale on the tourist map to work out the time of each journey. Could you walk or would you need to take the bus or drive in the car? Is there anywhere to park at each location? Could you visit all three places in one day?

Islands

Islands are pieces of land surrounded by water. Britain is made up of one very large island (consisting of Scotland, Wales and England) and more than 6,000 smaller islands, such as the Orkney and Shetland Islands, Anglesey, the Isles of Scilly and the Isle of Wight.

HARDER ROCK

Apart from the Isle of Wight, most of the islands are off the northern and western coasts of Britain where the rocks are harder and less likely to be worn away by the waves. Many of Britain's islands are important refuges for wildlife.

RISING SEA LEVELS

After the last Ice Age ended, about 10,000 years ago, rising temperatures and melting ice caused sea levels to rise (see pages 24–25). The main island of Britain was cut off from the rest of Europe and some of the land close to the shore became surrounded by the sea to form smaller islands.

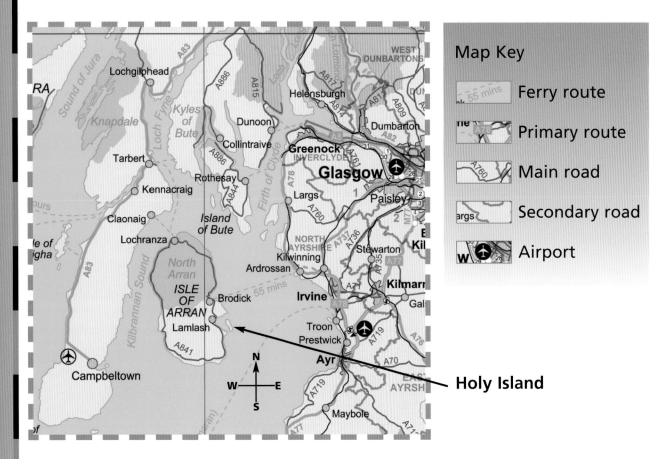

Map Key

Ferry route

Primary route

Main road

Secondary road

Airport

← **The west coast of Scotland is dotted with islands, including the Isle of Arran, which has another small island, called Holy Island, off its south-east coast, inside Lamlash Bay. Holy Island is only three kilometres in width, which is ten times smaller than the Isle of Arran.**

TAKING IT FURTHER

If you look up Holy Island in an atlas of Britain, you will find several islands have this name. To help you find the right island, it helps to know the numbers of a special set of imaginary lines, called latitude and longitude lines.

Lines of latitude go from side to side on a map and are parallel with the Equator (an imaginary line around the middle of the Earth). Lines of longitude go from top to bottom on a map. For this sort of reference, the latitude number is given first, followed by the longitude number.

The latitude and longitude reference for the Holy Island near Arran is: 55 31N and 5 4W. Can you find the latitude and longitude reference for the Holy Island off the north-east coast of England, near Berwick-on-Tweed? (This island is sometimes also called Lindisfarne.) Compare this reference with the one for the Holy Island off the coast of Anglesey in North Wales.

↓ Using the map

Travel maps
Look at the positions of the islands on the map. Which islands are furthest from the coast?

Look at the ferry routes. Which one is the longest route you can see? How different do you think island life is from mainland life?

Changing sea levels

The shape of Britain's coasts is being changed by rising sea levels and stronger, more frequent storms, which rapidly erode the coast.

↓ **Coasts have always changed. Milford Haven in Pembroke, Wales, was formed as a result of rising sea levels (or sinking of the land) flooding a river valley after the last Ice Age.**

CLIMATE CHANGE

Sea levels around the world rose between 1 mm and 2 mm a year during the 20th century. Many scientists think that during the 21st century, pollution of the atmosphere by gases such as carbon dioxide will trap more of the Sun's heat, melting glaciers and ice sheets to make the oceans expand. This climate change, some scientists say, may make sea levels rise faster than at any time in the past 100 years. By the 2080s, sea levels may be between 20 cm and 80 cm higher than they are today.

RISING AND SINKING

Sea level rises around Britain's coast will have different effects in the north and south. Northern Britain was covered with heavy ice during the last Ice Age, 70,000 to 10,000 years ago. Now the weight of the ice has gone, the land is gently rising. In contrast, much of southern Britain is sinking. This means that the south and east coasts of Britain are more likely to be flooded by rising sea levels.

THE EFFECTS OF RISING SEA LEVELS

- About 26 million people live in coastal towns and cities that might be flooded by rising sea levels.
- Many industrial sites are near the coast and would have to move inland.
- Over half of the best farmland in Britain is less than five metres above sea level and would be ruined if flooded with salty water.
- About 10 per cent of Britain's nature reserves are near the coast.
- Salty seawater mixing with freshwater near the coast would make some water supplies undrinkable.

TAKING IT FURTHER

Find out more about what different scientists think about climate change from the Internet, newspaper reports and television and radio programmes.

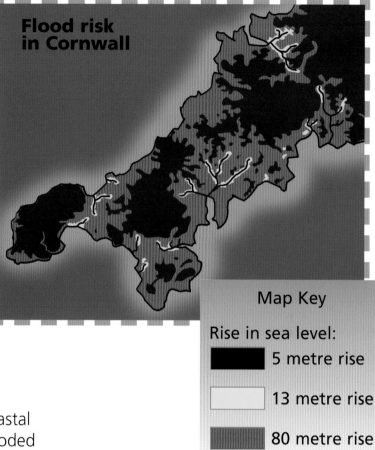

Flood risk in Cornwall

Map Key

Rise in sea level:

■ 5 metre rise

□ 13 metre rise

▓ 80 metre rise

↓ Using the map

Flood maps

Maps drawn on a computer can show areas at risk from rising sea levels. They can also show the new shape of the coastline if sea levels rose by different amounts. This helps geographers to explain their theories and give advice on the best ways of protecting the coast in the future. This map of Cornwall uses different colours to show the shape of the coast after three different sea level rises: 5 metre (500 years into the future), 13 metre (500–1,000 years) and 80 metre (melting of all ice).

Coastal management

Coasts have to be managed sustainably in different ways to balance the needs of people with the natural processes of erosion, deposition and flooding. Environmental issues such as rising sea levels only add to the many conflicts caused by coastal land use. Protecting coastlines is very expensive and is not always the best way to safeguard our shores for the future.

COASTAL CONFLICTS

Different groups of people want to use the coast in different ways.

- People who live on the coast want to keep their homes and protect the coastline.
- People who work on the coast want to use coastal resources, such as fish, oil, sand and stone.
- Tourists want free access to a clean, safe coastline.
- Environmental groups want to clean up pollution and preserve coastal habitats, especially those with rare plants and animals.

Local authorities have to look after the needs of the local people and try to solve conflicts between different groups.

↑ **Rock groynes at Mappleton, Yorkshire trap sand and stop it being swept along the coast by the waves. This also protects the cliffs from erosion. You can see the clay cliffs on the left of the photograph.**

TAKING IT FURTHER

See if you can find some newspaper reports of cliffs collapsing and homes falling into the sea, or make up an imaginary cliff collapse. Draw a map to show the old and new positions of the cliff. How would a map help to sort out conflicts between local people?

↓ Using the map

The Holderness coast east of Hull in Yorkshire is one of Europe's fastest eroding coastlines. The cliffs are formed from soft clay, which is easily worn away by the sea. Since Roman times, many villages and towns have disappeared under the waves.

This map shows the position of the Holderness coast in Roman times compared with the position of the present-day coastline.

Near the cliff-top village of Mappleton, south of Hornsea, the cliffs are eroding at a rate of two metres a year. In 1991, two types of hard engineering solutions were put in place: rock barriers (called groynes - see photo, left) and rock armour. The groynes protect the cliffs at Mappleton. However, the coast to the south of Mappleton is now being eroded more quickly than before because it no longer receives beach material to protect its cliffs. Farmers have lost land and homes. So solving a problem in one area of coast has caused more problems in another area.

A more sustainable way of managing the coast is called soft engineering. This system uses natural processes, such as adding sand to beaches, planting marshes or draining cliffs, to slow down coastal erosion without trying to stop it. It does not protect buildings or land, which makes it cheaper than hard engineering, although people may need to be paid compensation (money) for losing their land or homes.

Check your map skills

Use these two pages to check that you understand the mapping skills introduced in this book. Once you can read a map, you will be able to discover all sorts of information about coasts and how they change over time.

SCALE

Everything on a map is usually shrunk down by the same amount to fit onto the map. This is called drawing to scale. The scale of the map tells you how the size of the map compares to the size of the real landscape. You can use it to work out the actual size of the features on the map and the distances between two or more points.

GRIDS

A map grid is a network of equal squares drawn on top of the map. At the edge of the map, each line has a number or a letter at the end. To give a grid reference, find the numbers or letters at the ends of the two lines that meet in the bottom left-hand corner of a grid square. Refer to the line that goes up and down the map first, then the line that goes from side to side.

Look at the map

→ Look carefully at the map of Gorleston-on-Sea, which is near Great Yarmouth on the east coast of Norfolk. See if you can use your map skills to answer these questions.

→ What is the name of the beach nearest to the power station?

→ Give a grid reference to the square that contains the pier.

→ Where would a tourist go for help if they were taken ill on holiday?

→ Where is the best place to park if you want to visit Gorleston Cliffs?

→ What is the name of the monument just south of the Pleasure Beach?

→ How far is it from the Lifeboat Station to the Sea Life Centre?

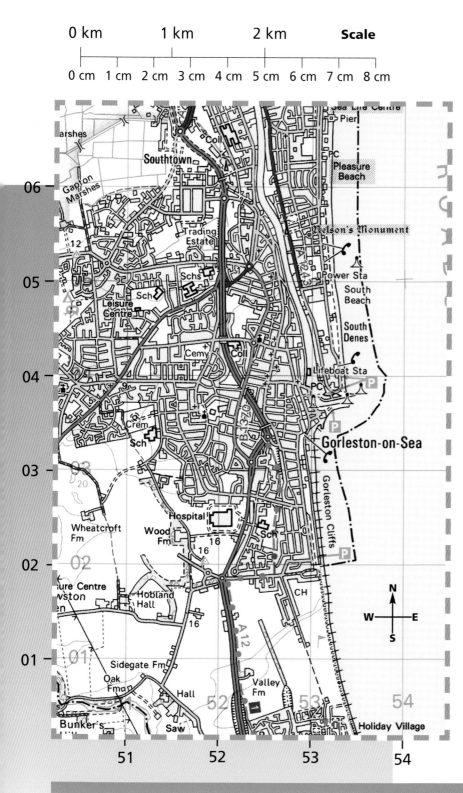

Scale

0 km   1 km   2 km

0 cm   1 cm   2 cm   3 cm   4 cm   5 cm   6 cm   7 cm   8 cm

SYMBOLS

Map symbols bring a map to life. They are simple signs that show where things are on a map. They may be small pictures, letters, shapes, lines or coloured areas that mark the position of features such as cliffs, beaches, woodlands, bus stations and paths. A list called a key or a legend on the edge of the map explains what the symbols stand for.

HEIGHT

The ups and downs of the land can be shown on a flat map by pictures of hills, shading, coloured areas or lines called hachures. The main way of showing height on a map is usually by contour lines. These are brown lines that join up places that are the same height above sea level. When the contours are close together, the land is steep. When the contours are far apart, the land is flatter. Rings of contours, one inside the other, show hills or mountains.

Map Key

 Telephone

 Church

Parking

County border

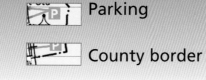 Footpath

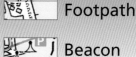 Beacon

Britain's coastline

This map shows areas of Britain's coast that are at risk from flooding due to rising sea levels and places particularly in danger of erosion. It also shows all the places mentioned in the book.

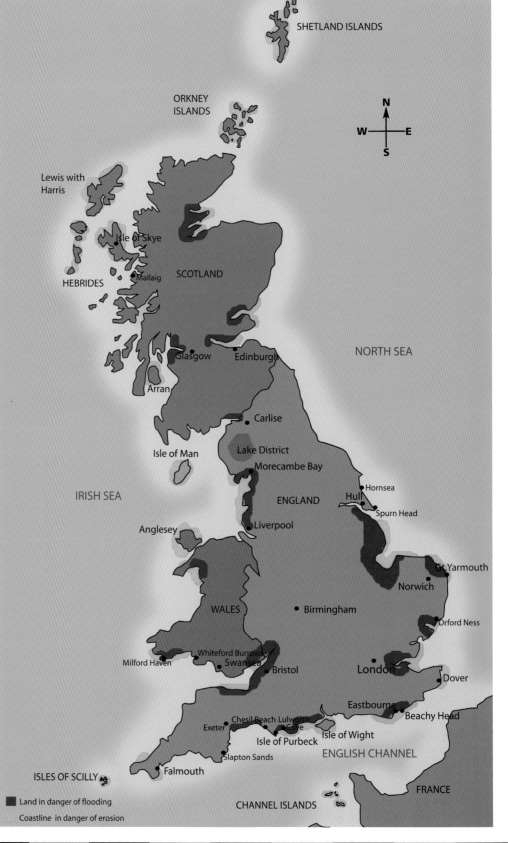

SHETLAND ISLANDS

ORKNEY ISLANDS

N
W   E
S

Lewis with Harris

Isle of Skye

HEBRIDES

Mallaig

SCOTLAND

NORTH SEA

Glasgow   Edinburgh

Arran

Carlise

Isle of Man

Lake District

Morecambe Bay

Hornsea

Hull

ENGLAND

Spurn Head

IRISH SEA

Liverpool

Anglesey

Gt.Yarmouth

Norwich

WALES   Birmingham

Orford Ness

Whiteford Burrows

Milford Haven   Swansea

Bristol

London

Dover

Eastbourne

Chesil Beach Lulworth Cove

Beachy Head

Exeter   Isle of Wight

Isle of Purbeck

Slapton Sands

ENGLISH CHANNEL

ISLES OF SCILLY   Falmouth

FRANCE

■ Land in danger of flooding

Coastline in danger of erosion

CHANNEL ISLANDS

Glossary

Aerial photograph A photograph taken from the sky looking down on the land.

Arch A bridge of rock, in which the weight of the centre is carried outwards and downwards to the ground.

Bar A ridge of sand or shingle across a bay on the coast, or a river mouth.

Bay An inward curve in the coastline with a headland on either side. A bay marks a place where softer rock has been worn away by the sea.

Beach A sloping band of sand, shingle or pebbles deposited along the coast by the action of the sea.

Cliff A slope or steep wall of rock and soil where the land meets the sea.

Climate change A significant change from one climatic condition to another such as the increase in the average temperature of the Earth's atmosphere.

Coast The boundary between the land and the sea.

Coastline The line on a map showing the position of the coast.

Contour A line on a map which joins places that are the same height above sea level.

Compass An instrument with a needle that points to magnetic North, which is used to find directions. It can be used with a map or on its own.

Erosion The loosening of rocks and soil and the carrying away of this material by the wind, water or ice.

Estuary The wide mouth of a river where freshwater in the river mixes with the salty water of the sea.

Geology map A map showing the rocks under the ground.

Grid lines Lines forming a network of squares on a map, which help to locate points easily and accurately.

Groynes Fence-like structures on a beach, which trap sand or pebbles and help to reduce longshore drift.

Hachures Short, thick lines used on a map to show the steepness and direction of slopes.

Harbour A place on the coast where ships can shelter, make repairs and take on fresh supplies.

Hard engineering Building structures to control geographical processes, such as coastal erosion.

Headland A piece of land that juts out into the sea.

Ice Age A very cold period in the Earth's history when more of the land was covered in ice. The last Ice Age (when ice covered most of Britain except southern areas) ended about 10,000 years ago.

Island An area of land surrounded by water on all sides.

Key A list that explains what the symbols on a map stand for. A key is sometimes called a legend because it tells the story of the map.

Lagoon A coastal lake cut off from the sea by a bar of sand or mud or a coral reef.

Lines of Latitude Imaginary lines forming a series of parallel circles around the Earth. They go from east to west (horizontally), spaced at regular intervals, both above and below the Equator, which is an imaginary line around the middle of the Earth.

Longshore drift The movement of beach material along the shore when the waves strike the coast at an angle.

Lines of Longitude Imaginary lines forming a series of circles round the Earth. They go from north to south (vertically), spaced at regular intervals, passing through the North and South Poles.

Marina A place where leisure boats are moored (tied up); not a place for working boats.

Ordnance Survey An organisation that makes accurate and detailed maps of the UK.

Peninsula A long neck of land ending in a headland.

Pollution The process of making the air, water or land dirty or poisonous, often because of waste produced by people.

Port A town or place with a harbour and the means for ships to load and unload their cargo.

Rock armour Large boulders piled on beaches, sometimes in steel mesh cages, to absorb some of the waves' energy and stop the coast being worn away.

Salt marsh A salt-water marsh formed on the coast where plants grow on areas of mud deposited in calm, shallow water.

Sand dune A mound of sand formed by the wind, which is found on the coast or in deserts.

Scale The particular size a map is drawn to.

Soft engineering Using natural environmental processes to cope with geographical problems, such as coastal erosion.

Spit A finger-like ridge of sand, shingle or mud, joined to the coast at one end, but extending out into the open sea. A spit is formed by longshore drift.

Stack A tall pillar of rock left behind when the sea cuts through a headland.

Sustainable Capable of being continued indefinitely.

Tide The rise and fall of the sea along the coast, which happens twice each day and is caused by the pull of the Moon and Sun's gravity and the spin of the Earth.

Tombolo A sand bridge linking an island with the mainland (the main part of a country, not the islands around it).

Index

FURTHER INFORMATION WEBSITES

Websites about coasts

www.fatbadgers.co.uk/Britain/coast.htm

www.bbc.co.uk/schools/riversandcoasts

www.bgs.ac.uk/education/makeamap/home.html

http://england.visualenc.com/dorset/geology_beach.html

www.morecambebay.com/maproom/wildlife.htm

www.welshwales.co.uk/historic_swansea.htm

www.vrweymouth.com

www.connexions.co.uk/areas/html/falmouth.html

www.bbc.co.uk/coast/programmes/13-highlights.shtml

Websites about maps

Ordnance Survey: www.ordnancesurvey.co.uk/mapzone

www.multimap.co.uk Type in place names or postcodes to see aerial views and maps of places in Britain.

Conservation organisations

National Parks Authorities: www.anpa.gov.uk

The National Trust: www.nationaltrust.org.uk

Environment Agency: www.environment-agency.gov.uk

The BBC's geography and natural history website: bbc.co.uk/nature

Note to parents and teachers: Every effort has been made by the Publishers to ensure that these websites are suitable for children, that they are of the highest educational value, and that they contain no inappropriate or offensive material. However, because of the nature of the Internet, it is impossible to guarantee that the contents of these sites will not be altered. We strongly advise that Internet access is supervised by a responsible adult.

These are the lists of contents for each title in
Mapping Britain's Landscapes:

Cities, Towns and Villages
What are cities, towns and villages? • Where do settlements grow up? • Settlements by rivers • Settlements by the sea • Mining and industry • Village life • Urban life • How do settlements grow and change? • Britain's capital • New developments • Getting about • Looking to the future • Check your map skills • Britain's towns and cities

Coasts
Mapping coasts • Wearing away coasts • Cliffs • Beaches and dunes • Changing shape • Where rivers meet coasts • Coastal settlements • Ports and harbours • Tourism and leisure • Islands • Changing sea levels • Coastal management • Check your map skills • Britain's coastline

Hills and Mountains
What are hills and mountains? • How do hills and mountains form? • Cliffs and block mountains • How are mountains shaped? • Worn by water • Sculpted by ice • Carved by glaciers • Farms and forests • Mining and energy Travel in hills • Towns and villages • Tourism and leisure • Check your map skills • Britain's mountains

Rivers
Mapping rivers • Rivers and the water cycle • How do rivers change the land? • Rivers in the highlands • Rivers in the lowlands • Where rivers meet the sea • When rivers flood • River settlements • Transport and crossing places • Water and work • Dams and reservoirs • Rivers and recreation Check your map skills • Britain's rivers